This book is for you if...

- you are contemplating transitioning from working full-time to easing into semi-retirement.

- you have made the decision to make the transition, and are trying to come up with a plan to make it happen.

- you would like to ensure that you make the transition with "eyes wide open".

- you are keen to learn from others who have made or are making this transition.

- you don't know what you don't know in terms of considering all the options open to you.

What people are saying

"David has the most incredible network and because he's worked with so many people over the years, he's genuinely more knowledgeable about dealing with you than anyone else I know. He makes it his business to care about and get under the skin of what you are doing so when you spend time with him, it's always constructive, helpfully challenging and therefore useful."
Lucy Standing, Founder and CEO – ViewVo

"David Mellor is a great coach and mentor. He is the archetypal networker, and is almost Delphic in his knowledge about setting up in business and how to grow that business. This booklet on semi-retirement will be fantastically helpful to all those who are embarking on a more portfolio existence and I cannot recommend it highly enough."
Andrew Pullman, CEO and Founder - People Risk Solutions

"I first met David in 2000 when he was Managing Director at Deutsche Bank eVentures – and therefore right in the heart of a big corporate beast. I was struck by his energy and enthusiasm.

"In the summer of 2001, David left Deutsche Bank and I left my own employer. By the end of 2001, I had set up the consultancy (Lysis Group) that I still run today and sought out David as an advisor and collaborator. Since then, David has been an ever-present part of the Lysis inner circle, first as Chairman and then as mentor and Advisory Panel chair. His counsel is always wise, he is always available to talk and I am honoured that, as he has gradually wound down some other commitments, he has remained close to Lysis.

"Which perhaps brings us to the point of this book: the move from full-time work for a major firm, to working for oneself, to part-time work and then retirement. I am tempted to say David is not very good at this because his enthusiasm drives him, but that would be wrong. He is actually very good at it and has worked out how to prioritise the wind-down so that the things he continues to do are the things that he finds most rewarding. I am not sure if his golf handicap is improving yet, but he seems to me to have achieved a good balance whereby he makes meaningful contributions to the work he has remained involved in and yet has more and more time for himself and his family. This book imparts some of his secrets."
Jon Sweet, CEO and Founder - Lysis Group

About the Author

Since 2001, David has developed a portfolio of activities which derive principally from 25 years' experience in commercial and investment banking with HSBC and Deutsche Bank. His consultancy activities embrace strategic planning and implementation, and mentoring existing and aspiring entrepreneurs. He is a recognised expert in his field, regularly speaking at conferences and running seminars and workshops. He provides one-on-one and group mentoring to aspiring entrepreneurs, many of whom are aiming to establish themselves as consultants.

He published *From Crew to Captain* in 2010, written for people making the transition from working for big institutions to working for themselves. He has followed that up by launching *From Crew to Captain: A Privateer's Tale* in 2014, which is written for people establishing consultancy practices.

The third book in the trilogy, *From Crew to Captain: Commander of the Fleet*, was released in November 2015 and addresses the "growing pains" issues faced by successful start-ups. All three books now exist in "bite-size" formats. He is also co-author of FT Publishing's *Inspirational Gamechangers* which launched in 2015.

He is an Honorary Senior Visiting Fellow in the Faculty of Finance at Cass Business School, where he has run workshops on managing strategic change, entrepreneurship, corporate entrepreneurship, leadership, building high performance teams, and sales. In addition, he has acted as course director and provided facilitation and mentoring support to participants in small groups and on a one-to-one basis.

David is a Freeman of the Guild of Entrepreneurs. He holds a Bachelor's and a Master's degree from the University of Cambridge, and is a Certified PRISM Brain Mapping Practitioner.

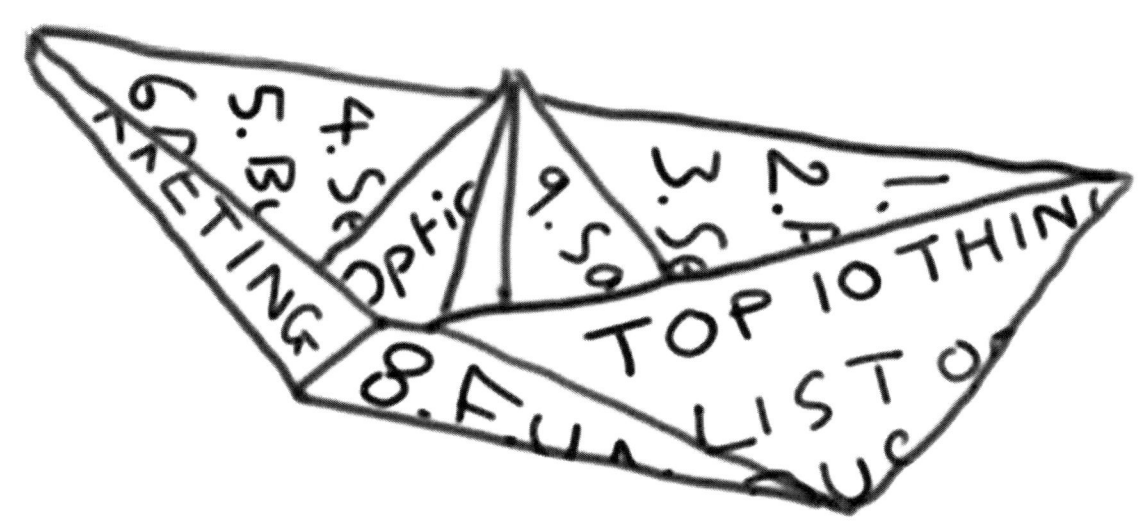

From Crew to Captain

Changing Tack

Making the transition from working full-time to semi-retirement

by David Mellor

with illustrations by James Mellor

Published by Filament Publishing Ltd

16 Croydon Road, Waddon, Croydon,

Surrey, CR0 4PA, United Kingdom

Telephone +44(0)20 8688 2598

info@filamentpublishing.com

www.filamentpublishing.com

ISBN 978-1-913192-85-3

Printed by 4edge Ltd.

A quick word from David Mellor...

The purpose of this little book is to help people understand the realities of trying to transition from working full-time to achieving genuine semi-retirement. I am making this journey myself, and just wanted to share with other people what it is really like.

I have selected 30 lessons that I have learned thus far, and tried to balance what I have experienced with observations from 30 other people. I am extremely grateful to them all. My key objective is to present you with an opportunity to move forward with confidence and "eyes wide open".

I hope that the list (and if you have read any of my other books, you will know that I love lists!) will help to inform your reflection, planning and resultant activity.

If the list creates a desire to dive deeper on some of the topics, then please feel free to contact me at david@davidmellormentoring.com or on 07957 480460.

Additional copies of the book can be purchased from my website:
www.davidmellormentoring.com

Speed Dial

The "Speed Dial" Option

- How do I deal with Time Management? Jump to page 14

- What should I do in terms of Marketing and Sales? Jump to page 28

- What should my client strategy be? Jump to page 36

- What should my network look like? Jump to page 42

- How do I go about revenue generation? Jump to page 46

- What about cost reduction initiatives? Jump to page 52

- How do I manage non-work days? Jump to page 56

- What else do I need to know? Jump to page 70

A List of Lists - Contents

**"You need to make this transition 'eyes wide open',
as opposed to 'eyes wide shut'."**

TIME MANAGEMENT

Lesson 1

Don't try to cram five days' work into three. Doesn't work.

Retain what you enjoy, turn your work into a hobby, embrace the passion, become a mentor, give back to the industry pro-bono, advise and help. There is still so much you can do.

David Meynell

Lesson 2

Block non-working days in your diary so that the wrong stuff doesn't go in.

I'm finally working at a pace I enjoy!

Joella Bruckshaw

Lesson 3

Being in your office at home doesn't count as a non-working day.

My prime memory of semi-retirement (i.e. giving up executive life for advisory/NED work) is you go from the shelter of the Corporate umbrella to the management of your personal brand.

On the personal front, you have to develop a new approach to life with your partner given the change of work and lifestyle.

It's your change, not your partner's.

Brian Stevenson

Lesson 4

Don't fret if you have a genuine free day. Relax and enjoy it.

I was looking forward to giving up work but realised I still had a couple of grey cells working and needed the stimulation of business.

It's great playing golf, going on holiday and watching the grass grow when retired, but you need to keep active, and working in business can still be such fun.

If you are still active and not completely switched off from business, it is a shame if you cannot pass on those "pearls of wisdom" you have gathered over the years.

If you can still communicate, make sense without dribbling and people are still listening, then it would be a shame to give up working completely.

Becoming semi-retired has major benefits as you can have greater control of your time and keep involved in business and the assignments you want to take on.

Dick Haynes

Lesson 5

Be discerning in your decisions around what work/assignments to continue; it's what you want to do that counts.

Fill your new target spare time with things you want to do (non-work related) so you do them! For example, holidays, learning something new...

Colin Spiller

Lesson 6

Consider how much time and money (if any) you want to spend on marketing, particularly if the ROI has traditionally been low.

In my case, semi-retirement has been wonderful! However, some planning is definitely needed - my recommendation to anyone who has this milestone coming up is to hire a coach to talk through all the elements: financial, ego, relationships, and so on.

Diane King

Lesson 7

Review any committee positions and decide whether to continue or step down.

I advise clients who are heading into semi-retirement to review, reframe and relaunch their personal PSB - purpose, strategy and behaviour plan - to suit their new context and not try to shoehorn their old PSB into what is effectively a "start-up", albeit in later life.

Ciaran Fenton

MARKETING AND SALES

Lesson 8

Review the range of networking groups you belong to and assess whether any of them will be a good use of your time and money going forward. If not, then plan to exit gracefully.

I have been through this process over the last five years. The hardest thing that I found was attempting to refocus from a busy lifestyle and the self-importance that goes with it, to a new lifestyle where you are almost invisible. The phones stop ringing, people don't seek your advice and the world carries on quite happily without you! The art of the negotiator lies idle whilst the world moves on.

I was fortunate enough to get involved as a mentor and share my experiences with new businesses for mutual benefit, and my lifestyle has taken a rather different turn. To be a successful retiree, one has to re-learn how to fit into a totally different world and adapt to the new circumstances. I never missed the business itself for one moment, but the constant drip of unneeded experience into the bin was another matter.

Now I enjoy life to the full helping others, but particularly myself. Business is now fun and a matter for obtaining maximum enjoyment as one's objectives become less P&L and balance sheet-orientated, and more a stress-free social adventure.

Richard Remmer

Lesson 9

Think twice before you go chasing new business or following up.

This is part wishful thinking and part a tax/pensions play. I haven't really noticed that I've moved to self-retirement.

Professor Cliff Oswick

Lesson 10

Not every client is a good client. Decide which ones you want to retain and which ones you want to "ease out".

I now really look forward to my one day of paid work per week. It's a welcome relief from the endless unpaid hours spent in the house and garden, plus I get to look super smart at least one day a week.

Christine Ward

Lesson 11

Review any Non-Executive Director positions and decide whether to continue or step down.

Ironically, trying to go part-time has led to a promotion which means I am, for the moment, doing full-time plus.

Professor Stephen Thomas

CLIENTS

Lesson 12

Make sure you allocate time to nurture your core client set, and don't take them for granted.

The retirement age thing really is just a number! The key for me is how you see your life and finding work that really gives you a sense of purpose and uses your talents and experience – it's all too easy to lose your sense of identity in retirement.

Dr. Roger Greene

Lesson 13

Be selfish with your time. Rid yourself of the time-wasters and the discourteous.

Semi-retirement for me has been about portfolio project management. It has been about embracing the fact that all my "employment" eggs are not in one basket. Early on, I recognised I did not want to average more than a three-day week (so that I was only truly part-time) but that I wanted to be more than a non-executive to the companies I worked with so that I could fully immerse myself in their businesses. Therefore, I knew I would limit the number of roles to less than three at any one time. The primary skills associated with this kind of employment lifestyle are about digesting the detail but being alive to the risks and opportunities, reading around your company and its position in the marketplace, and being able to delegate and finding the key question/decision at all times. Ensuring there are good people working full-time around you has also been important.

Many people recommend finding an outside interest, keeping busy at all times. My personal observation is to protect your downtime. If, like me, you like exercise, then use the extra time but do not slavishly fill your day. The attraction of working less hard is being able to feel sometimes you do not have a hundred things to do! Go to that museum, see a film during the working day, walk in the woods, relax more, and keep pressing those knowledge boundaries.

One final item. Many are attracted by doing something they are familiar with. I have taken on roles that utilise my skill set but also when selecting, I have been attracted by those that give me new challenges. You can and should still learn in semi-retirement.

Tony Westlake

Lesson 14

If you don't have them already, set yourself some client adoption criteria, and don't depart from them.

Avoid the 'R' word like the plague. It immediately puts you in a daytime telly/doing the gardening/taking up golf mindset, some or all of which are liable to be short-term diversions. Instead, join a local business networking group. It will keep you in touch with younger people who may value your experience, in particular how to maximise opportunities and avoid problems.

And keep yourself in the market. There will be people happy to pay you to work on a consultancy or part-time basis. Great for topping up the pension!

Richard Harvey

NETWORKS

Lesson 15

Make sure that you have the network of individuals you need for your new modus operandi.

My wonderful father first retired at 65 but missed the joy of work, so he returned to the family business before finally retiring at 90!

He was a wine merchant and taught me a thing or two about leading a balanced lifestyle and taking a work-related hobby with him into retirement, steadily enjoying drinking the best fruits of the vine and well-earned profits.

That is a precedent I feel duty bound to follow but I still have to work out how to achieve the 25 years of sufficient profits to allow me to do the same.

Miles Smith

Lesson 16

Be very discerning about whom you want to retain in your "inner circle" network. Set criteria for "admission" to your core network, then nurture the chosen few.

Some advance planning is important but you might prefer first to have some downtime to reflect rather than "hitting the ground running". Life is not going to be the same and you should not try to replicate what you had and desperately try to fill all your time. The joy is having more time to enjoy personal interests and hobbies, and to have more time with family and friends and to repair neglected relationships, as well as an opportunity to give back to society in a variety of ways.

Whilst you might not be the "boss" in a corporate environment, you are more in control of your life and can structure a work/life balance that makes you happy most of the time, rather than some of the time. Remain flexible and open-minded and be ready to consider opportunities that were not part of your original plan. That being said, be selective and don't take on work and commitments just to fill time or to persuade your former colleagues that you are busy. The truth is, they are envious!

Alan Elias

REVENUE

Lesson 17

Consider what ways you could possibly "make money in your sleep".

We are a husband and wife team running an IT company and we spent about three years planning our exit strategy and working out what it was we actually wanted from life. Our exit strategy is now not to exit! The thought of counting how many steps the postman takes up our garden path each day was too scary.

We instead grew a little and brought in new employees to replace the day-to-day work we did so we aren't part of "production". We rethought our company's Vision & Mission and worked on the company culture. The team now want the company to grow so we are more involved than ever but crucially we are able to take time out for other activities while maintaining a sense of purpose; I've taken up Tai Chi and I'm learning to play the guitar.

The other thing that came out of the process is that we realised we aren't very good at blue sky thinking, we are much better at making other people's ideas happen.

Melanie and Chris Ball

Lesson 18

Ask yourself the question, "Have I got a book in me, or two, or three...?"

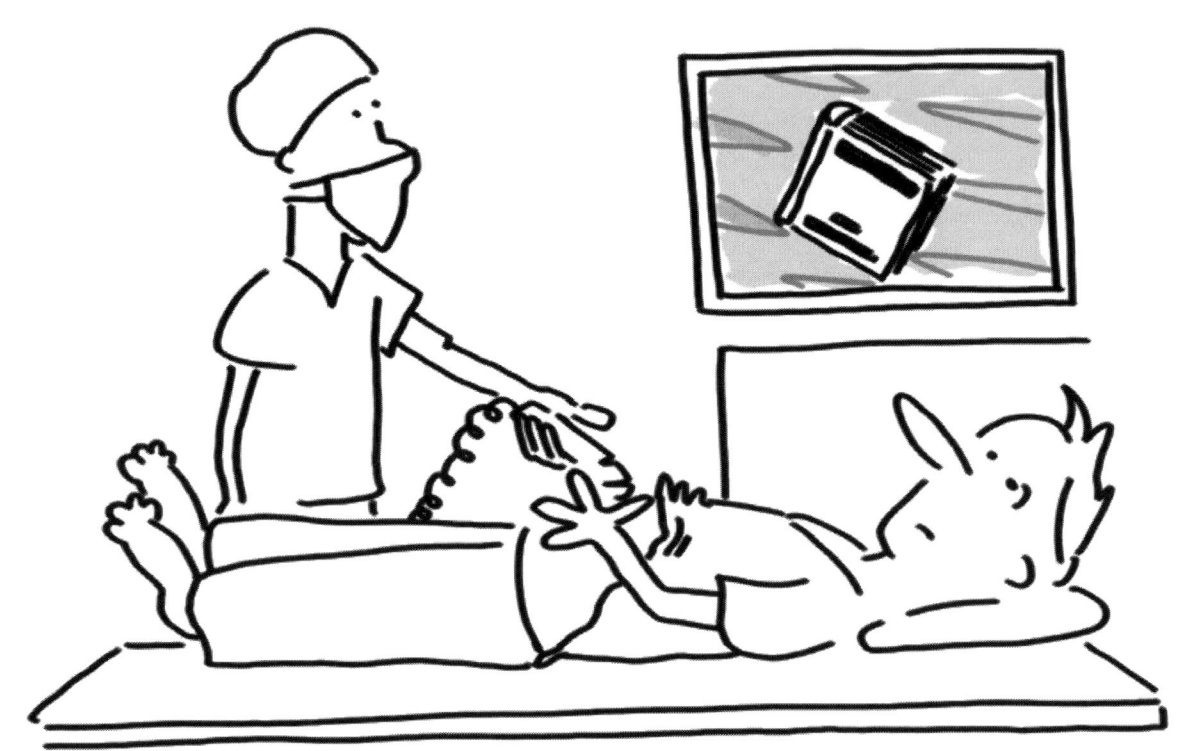

From my observations of those that have retired, or proceeded to semi-retirement, there are three key factors which will determine how well you enjoy your retirement. Firstly, ensuring financial provision; secondly, maintaining a sense of value; thirdly, exercising control:

- On financial provision - a good pension is key.

- On maintaining a sense of value - supplementing your pension with income from fee-earning work is important for building that 'sense of value' and keeping the mind and body active.

- Ensuring that you have control over when and where you work.

Dermot Hill

Lesson 19

Take the opportunity to review your pricing model and explore the validity of easing it upwards.

As I am still in the process of extricating myself from my long-term employer, the first thing that comes to mind is that my decision to step down from full-time employment has been surprisingly stressful. The irony that a decision to downsize work should lead to an uptick in stress is not lost on me, but leaving behind a lifetime's work, executive life, a business, colleagues and friends is, of course, a big decision, so don't be surprised if you find yourself soul-searching, writing lists of pros and cons, and thinking about little else. I certainly have been taken by surprise, and it has meant the counsel of friends, family, and especially people who have done the same thing has been invaluable.

I would also observe that there is no rush to fill your days immediately. The things you want to do with your time, apart from things like travel, hobbies or gardening, may not be immediately obvious and some ideas take time to evolve, so give yourself that time and don't feel pressure to be going straight into something else. Time is now on your side.

Simon Sayer

COSTS

Lesson 20

If you are reducing your working hours by 40%, and are assuming a drop in revenue of 40%, have you figured out how to reduce your costs by an equivalent amount?

My observations of friends/people that I know that have 'retired' indicates that it is rather like Marmite … they either loved it or hated it!

Those that have planned for retirement and have the funds to enjoy it, have tended to. Those where compulsory 'retirement' has been thrust upon them, or who have financial issues or no one to spend the time with, have often found it a real struggle. Lack of purpose and self-worth is a big issue!

Entrepreneurs seem to find it particularly difficult to 'retire' fully and often find themselves another opportunity or two to run with. I am not sure if true entrepreneurs ever retire!

Judy Hadden

Lesson 21

Come up with a cost reduction programme and action it – separate the necessary from the discretionary.

Embark on a project, activity or business which suits your likes and skills; not necessarily your previous career. Grasp the opportunity to follow your dream if you can. I was astounded at the number of people who stated they wished they could have had the same opportunity. In truth, many did have the opportunity but avoided the risk.

Expect your time to be fully employed irrespective of your choice of future activities. Your inability to attend social functions will be regularly challenged with the phrase "I thought you were taking it easy now".

I missed the opportunities to discuss things with colleagues. I found that making the effort to discuss things with friends and family helped keep the internalisation of problems at bay. However, it did take some time to get to that point.

It may transpire that you feel guilty for deserting your close working team. My ex-colleagues adjusted far quicker than I did.

It can take some time to adjust to a new regime. It took me many months to restructure my life into a rewarding routine.

Do not rush into a project, activity or interest unless you are convinced it is for you. Breaking away from the wrong choice can be difficult. You may find that failure to follow your initial commitment can damage your reputation and friendships. It is all too easy to jump at the first opportunity when faced with relative inactivity.

Dave Evans

NON-WORK DAYS

Lesson 22

If you have created a non-work day, plan ahead and make sure you know how you want to use it, so you don't get tempted to slip some work stuff in.

In 2000, my 25-year headhunting career in international banking hit the buffers. Aged 50, I had leukaemia. A bone marrow transplant was scheduled but, at the eleventh hour, I was admitted to the clinical trial of a new drug. In 2003, the medics gave me the 'all clear': the drug had worked! I had been on sick leave for three years. So, what next?

Back in 2001, my wife and I had decided to move from Surrey to a new, but smaller, property in West Sussex. The move would release enough money to maintain our lifestyle until our pensions became payable in 2010. It would also leave my wife with some free capital were I to die and, were I to live, the scope for me to try something new without heavy financial pressures.

Following my 'all clear' in 2003, I decided not to revive my dormant headhunting career. I had a very different business venture in mind.

The idea had stemmed from our 'downsizing' project two years earlier. This had (somewhat predictably!) left us short of storage space. The solution was our double garage in which we quickly installed a large-capacity and high-quality garage shelving system. Our new shelving was much admired by neighbours and I thought, even then, that one could build a business around garage shelving.

Trading as 'The Garage Shelving Service', my new venture in 2003 set out to build that business. Target customers would be families who had recently bought new, 4/5 bedroom properties. The 'service' provided would be to design, supply and install bespoke garage shelving arrangements for customers, giving them 'a place for everything' in their new homes.

Since 2003, I have thoroughly enjoyed delivering the service as described and making an attractive profit margin on each project. I'm self-employed, have very low fixed overheads, work single-handed and am not financially dependent on income from the business. I set my own pace and take breaks when it suits me.

Gary Gibbons

Lesson 23

Continue to invest in your own personal development, so that you keep up to date with the latest developments and requirements in your chosen sector(s).

Having joined the world of insurance from leaving school, I found myself 40 years later being the Chairman of the UK business for an international broker with responsibility for 18 UK offices, employing over 700 staff and an annual brokerage of £40m.

I had a "Life Plan" to retire from full-time corporate life at 57, which I did.

However, a number of companies contacted me to ask if I was interested in working with them to support their endeavours and fairly quickly I became self-employed. Seven years later, I am now working with a number of organisations as either a Non-Executive Director or by providing advice on a wide range of management subjects.

It has been a great opportunity to harness and deploy all of the learning that I gained from my "Corporate" life and hopefully I continue to provide useful insight to a wonderful Industry.

Paul Smith

Lesson 24

If you are taking a few days off, try to keep the day after your return free so that you can ease yourself back in and catch up without undue stress.

Semi-retirement is a dramatic readjustment of one's work/life balance. Many feel it comes about through considered choice but not in my experience. I found myself in an untenable political situation with an employer after years of running my own companies and had to resign and walk away.

So there I was, with insufficient pension and savings provision, too old and out of touch to find a "regular job", but too young and unprepared to retire.

I had insufficient board-level experience to take the NED route, and little appetite or funding to create a brand new business in my chosen field from scratch.

In the end, I took some time off and cleared my head, took the advice of friends and family and decided to re-evaluate my skills and talents and look at fresh opportunities that would combine my unfulfilled dreams and strong passions, finding a platform where I could make a difference.

And for me, once I had shortlisted business ideas, prospective ventures seemed to emerge from friends and business contacts from my past - the little black book in action. They knew me and that took the pressure off having to apply and validate myself afresh.

It's been a year since I walked away from full-time work and only now, the shape of my semi-retirement is emerging enough that I can balance the needs of income to leisure and hobby time etc. Also, being in a fairly recent relationship affects my future plans and requirements. Plus, weddings to pay for impact one's finances.

Key for me was always a wish to keep my eye in the game business-wise rather than playing golf all day. I am sure charitable work will be factored in somewhere too once my now grown-up kids are settled enough to be able to support me in my dotage!

Chris Parkes

Lesson 25

If you are not doing it already, consider doing some pro-bono work and give something back to the community.

You need to plan ahead, three to five years ahead, of leaving your full-time role.

Get your network message on what it is you are planning to do or not do next.

The fastest way to dementia for anyone is to stop working. Like all muscles, brains need to be exercised regularly

You need to know what you love doing, and spend your retirement doing just that.

It's often quoted, find a job you love and you'll never work again. Well, find something you love to do, and you'll never retire.

That said, you need to understand the value you bring to an organisation, because it's that value they will retain/remunerate. It's not sufficient to be something you want to do, they have to have a need for it.

Michael Moran

Lesson 26

Think about developing an existing interest or skill.

I expected one of the biggest challenges to be getting out and networking as this wasn't something that came naturally to me. In practice, I found it easier than expected and people have been genuinely welcoming and helpful towards getting me started.

Interestingly, some of the key contacts that I was hopeful of gaining work through have not necessarily been my best prospects in reality. Conversely, some of the most chance meetings have led to significant opportunities so one always needs to approach things with an open mind.

Compared to my initial expectations, the consultancy work has actually been less forthcoming. To some extent, this reflects that most of the opportunities seem to be London-focused. After not too many months out in the big world, I reflected that actually part of my reason for leaving full-time permanent employment was to get a better work-life balance, and living out of a suitcase in London didn't really deliver this. So, I have focused my efforts on seeking opportunities in the north, particularly the Yorkshire area. I have also secured more non-exec appointments. Although these took time to materialise, they provide a more long-term sustainable income.

On the mentoring side, I now have four clients, although one sadly has been made redundant. I find the work is mentally challenging but also rewarding to help individuals on their journey.

LinkedIn and following my own contact network, including attending networking lunches (I joined the Chamber of Commerce locally and have taken up the Chair of the property forum), trade conferences and things like Angel pitching sessions, have been the most fruitful ways of generating new opportunities.

Anon

Lesson 27

Think about taking up a new interest or developing a new skill.

"Having a sense of purpose has made my retirement more meaningful and kept the grey matter working well."

"Having fun is a lifelong activity - not something that's reserved for the young alone."

"Having enough money is good, but having the right content in your life is loads better."

"Retirement has given me time to evolve."

Various anon (contributed by Paul Jones)

Lesson 28

Think about how you could structure your week to create more long weekends.

I'm working on reducing my number of days per week, but I have so many bits and pieces of work (an hour here, an hour there...) I'm not sure how successful I am!

Tracey Bowles

"ODD SOCK DRAWER"

Lesson 29

Create a set of business and personal objectives that you can review and measure monthly.

Moving from corporate civvy street to entrepreneurial maverick comes with both its joys and challenges. You are effectively moving from the bosom of mothership, where they feed you, pay you, performance-manage you and, depending on the company you work for, even give you a massage on a Friday afternoon (!), to... frankly, eating what you kill! Suddenly, there is no legal support, no payroll, no HR, no IT support... everything that you have always taken for granted! But the sense of achievement in making it in the wild makes it all worthwhile! It makes you feel a million dollars... even if your company bank account tells you otherwise!

Mark Savage

Lesson 30

Don't put off doing things when you have time to do them – seize the moment.

The temptation in the early days following the start of part-time working is to check emails and it is so hard not to respond to them – don't. Not only will this confuse your colleagues/customers but also defeats the whole object of the transition process.

Launch your plans on what you intend to do with your days off immediately from day one of working part-time. If you haven't got a plan, set one up now. Otherwise, you will just drift during your day off and achieve nothing – unless that is your objective!

Manage expectations – do not be afraid to tell people that you are working part-time and that actions/responses will have to wait until you are back in the office. One piece of advice that I received in the early days was to put my Out of Office message on my emails to say "Not working today" – I took that advice and it has worked well for all.

When you transit to part-time working, you save on transport costs, lunches, coffees, impulse buys and after work drinks, so avoid the substitution of new costly expenditure on your days off. Investment in new activities need not be expensive.

Stanley Nonis

FROM CREW TO CAPTAIN (Book 1)
Making the transition from working for a big institution
to working for yourself
By David Mellor
with original illustrations by James Mellor

The purpose of this book is to help people understand the transition from working for a big institution to working for themselves. I have made this journey, and helped many others do the same. I want to put the odds in your favour, if you decide to follow suit, that your business venture brings you everything you wish, and that you prosper rather than merely survive. You will find inside a number of practical tips and hints, all garnered from the "University of Life".

I will draw on a broad range of interview material from people who have made or are making this journey, and for whom success has looked very different. It will also draw on a wealth of anecdotal evidence, from my own experience and that of others.

Our journey will take us through three important phases:

1. Reflecting - what does it take to make this transition - and is it for you?

2. Planning - how do you go about preparing to launch your business?

3. Doing - what attributes are going to be really important in the early days post launch?

This book is for you if...

- you have always wondered about what running your own business would be like.

- you are prepared to admit you don't know what you don't know.

- you wonder whether you have personally "got what it takes".

- you think you have an idea but you don't know whether it is commercially viable.

- you are unsure what business skills you will need.

- you don't know what a business plan needs to look like.

- you don't know where to start in terms of raising money.

- you have heard of marketing but are not entirely sure what it is and why you would need it.

- you find the idea of selling scary or daunting.

- you want to put the odds in your favour so that if you do decide to start a business, it will be successful.

FROM CREW TO CAPTAIN: A PRIVATEER'S TALE (Book 2)
by David Mellor
with original illustrations by James Mellor

The user-friendly guide to launching and growing a successful consultancy business.

When you're launching your own business, there's nothing like friendly, straightforward advice to set you on the right course. My book *From Crew To Captain: A Privateer's Tale* takes sound business advice and delivers it in a jargon-free, conversational style, making it that rarest of beasts: a business book that is both informative and enjoyable to read!

As a consultant and mentor, since 2001 I have helped scores of people successfully launch their own business. My first book, *From Crew To Captain*, guided aspiring entrepreneurs through the transition from being part of a big institution to working for themselves.

From Crew To Captain: A Privateer's Tale is designed to help people take the next steps of their journey as they launch and, with any luck, grow their new practice. The easy-to-absorb advice and tips are interspersed with useful checklists and light-hearted illustrations as well as one or two cautionary anecdotes!

Drawing from my own successful career as a consultant and through interviews with colleagues, peers and mentees, *From Crew To Captain: A Privateer's Tale* delivers honest, pragmatic advice and offers a simple but highly effective framework that will help consultants from almost any sector maximise their chances of developing a profitable, successful business.

This book is for you if...

- you are contemplating, or in the process of, a career change, be it planned or enforced.

- you would like to make money out of what you have learned in your career to date.

- you want to understand how to set up a sole practitioner consultancy practice or similar.

- you don't know what you don't know in terms of making the transition successfully.

- you would like to know more about what "good consultancy" looks like.

- you need help in addressing how to sell consultancy services.

- you are keen to achieve "client delight" through your delivery.

- you would welcome someone going on the journey with you.

FROM CREW TO CAPTAIN: COMMANDER OF THE FLEET (Book 3)
by David Mellor
with original illustrations by James Mellor

This book completes a trilogy. Book 1 (*From Crew to Captain*) addressed how to make the transition from working for a big institution to working for yourself. Book 2 (*A Privateer's Tale*) looked specifically at how to set up as a sole practitioner consultant or similar.

The purpose of this book is to help people who have set up their own business, proved to themselves and the market that their model works, and are looking to take it to the next level. I have made this journey, and helped many others do the same.

As with the first two books, you will find inside a number of practical tips and hints, all garnered from the "University of Life".

We will look at four important aspects of early business growth:

1. Assessing the Situation - what does the business look like today, and why do you want to change it?

2. Achieving Transformation - how do you go about creating and implementing a change strategy?

3. Assessing the Outcome – how do you evaluate success?

4. Building a Consultancy Practice – how do you move from a sole practitioner to a multi-consultant practice?

You may be wondering why I decided to put pen to paper again having written the first two books. One of the issues, which is important to me, is closure. I don't like loose ends, and I had a sense that the first two books left some "unfinished business". I knew I wouldn't rest easy until I had dealt with it by writing Book 3.

So, this book picks up the journey from where the first two books left off. My personal sub-title for the book is "Growing pains and how to deal with them", because that is exactly what the book addresses. Whatever type of business you are trying to build, I hope you will find some "gold nuggets" there.

This book is for you if...

- you have an existing business.

- you have proved to yourself and the market that your business model works.

- you want to understand how to take the business to the next level.

- you don't know what you don't know in terms of making the transition successfully.

- you would like to know more about how to create a value business capable of sustainable profitable growth.

- as a specific issue, you need help in addressing how you move from a sole practitioner model to running a multi-consultant practice.

- you would welcome someone going on the journey with you.